PIANO · VOCAL · GUITAR

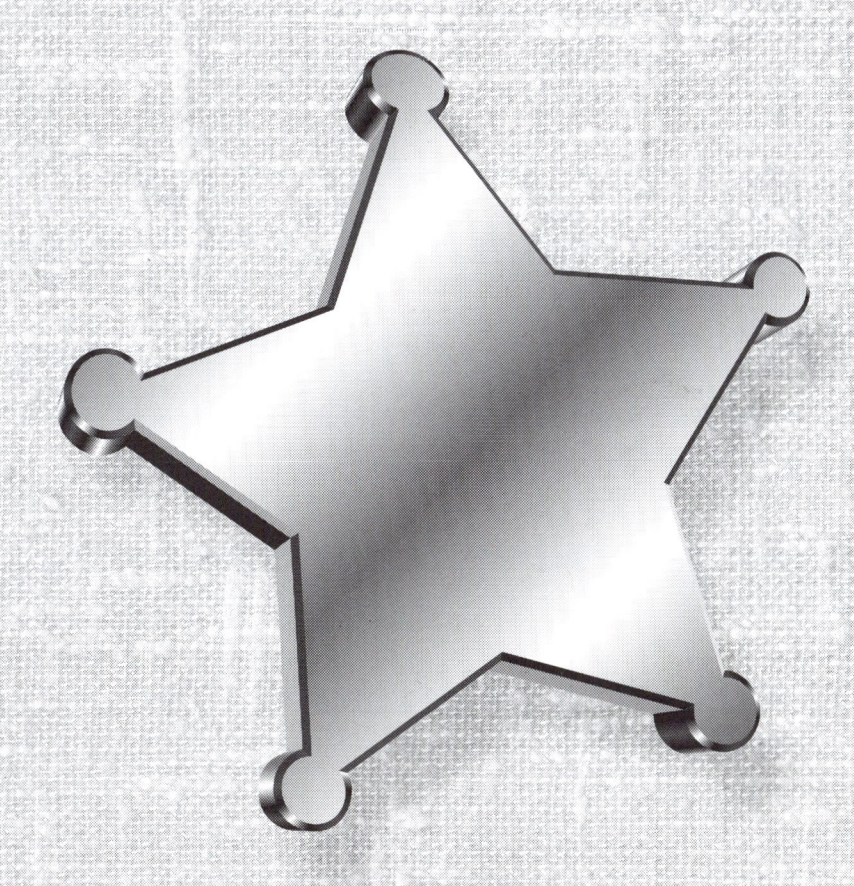

NEW COUNTRY STARS
OF THE '90s
32 Hits • 32 Stars

This publication is not for sale in
the E.C. and/or Australia
or New Zealand.

ISBN 0-7935-5951-0

HAL•LEONARD CORPORATION
7777 W. BLUEMOUND RD. P.O.BOX 13819 MILWAUKEE, WI 53213

Copyright © 1996 by HAL LEONARD CORPORATION
International Copyright Secured   All Rights Reserved

For all works contained herein:
Unauthorized copying, arranging, adapting, recording or public performance is an infringement of copyright.
Infringers are liable under the law.

Contents

Rhett Akins That Ain't My Truck 128

John Berry Standing on the Edge of Goodbye 117

Clint Black Untanglin' My Mind 149

Brooks & Dunn You're Gonna Miss Me When I'm Gone 166

Garth Brooks Friends in Low Places 36

Tracy Byrd The Keeper of the Stars 76

Kenny Chesney Fall in Love 26

Mark Chesnutt She Dreams 122

Mark Collie Even the Man in the Moon Is Cryin' 20

Billy Ray Cyrus Achy Breaky Heart (Don't Tell My Heart) 10

Billy Dean If There Hadn't Been You 62

Diamond Rio In a Week or Two 72

Joe Diffie If the Devil Danced (In Empty Pockets) 57

Faith Hill Let's Go to Vegas 86

Alan Jackson Gone Country 42

Toby Keith You Ain't Much Fun 172

Sammy Kershaw If You're Gonna Walk, I'm Gonna Crawl 67

Tracy Lawrence Texas Tornado 144

Little Texas Life Goes On 81

The Mavericks There Goes My Heart 134

Terry McBride & The Ride Sacred Ground 112

Neal McCoy No Doubt About It 97

Tim McGraw Refried Dreams 107

John Michael Montgomery I Can Love You Like That 47

Collin Raye One Boy, One Girl 102

Doug Stone Too Busy Being in Love 140

Doug Supernaw What'll You Do About Me 154

Aaron Tippin Working Man's Ph.D. 161

Rick Trevino Bobbie Ann Mason 16

Travis Tritt Foolish Pride 30

Clay Walker My Heart Will Never Know 92

Trisha Yearwood I Wanna Go Too Far 52

Contents Alphabetical by Song Title

Achy Breaky Heart
(Don't Tell My Heart) 10

Bobbie Ann Mason 16

Even the Man in
the Moon is Cryin' 20

Fall in Love 26

Foolish Pride 30

Friends in Low Places............ 36

Gone Country 42

I Can Love You Like That 47

I Wanna Go Too Far............. 52

If the Devil Danced
(In Empty Pockets) 57

If There Hadn't Been You........ 62

If You're Gonna Walk,
I'm Gonna Crawl 67

In a Week or Two............... 72

The Keeper of the Stars 76

Let's Go to Vegas................ 86

Life Goes On.................... 81

My Heart Will Never Know 92

No Doubt About It 97

One Boy, One Girl............... 102

Refried Dreams 107

Sacred Ground 112

She Dreams 122

Standing on the Edge
of Goodbye 117

Texas Tornado 144

That Ain't My Truck............. 128

There Goes My Heart 134

Too Busy Being in Love.......... 140

Untanglin' My Mind............. 149

What'll You Do About Me 154

Working Man's Ph.D. 161

You Ain't Much Fun 172

You're Gonna Miss Me
When I'm Gone................. 166

Complete History of Charted Singles

As of 2/96. Dates given are the month the single first appeared on the chart.

RHETT AKINS

I Brake for Brunettes (1/95)
She Said Yes (10/95)
That Ain't My Truck (5/95)
What They're Talkin' About (10/94)

JOHN BERRY

A Mind of Her Own (6/93)
I Think About It All the Time (7/95)
If I Had Any Pride Left at All (10/95)
Kiss Me in the Car (9/93)
Standing on the Edge of Goodbye (3/95)
What's in It for Me (6/94)
You and Only You (10/94)
Your Love Amazes Me (2/94)

CLINT BLACK

A Bad Goodbye (with Wynonna) (5/93)
Better Man (2/89)
Burn One Down (9/92)
Desperado (10/93)
A Good Run of Bad Luck (3/94)
Half the Man (6/94)
Hold on Partner (with Roy Rogers) (11/91)
The Kid (1/96)
Killin' Time (7/89)
Life Gets Away (10/95)
Loving Blind (2/91)
No Time to Kill (8/93)
Nobody's Home (11/89)
Nothing's News (7/90)
One Emotion (7/95)
One More Payment (4/91)
Put Yourself in My Shoes (10/90)
State of Mind (11/93)
Summer's Comin' (4/95)
This Nightlife (4/92)
Tuckered Out (2/94)
Untanglin' My Mind (9/94)
Walkin' Away (3/90)
We Tell Ourselves (6/92)
When My Ship Comes In (1/93)
Where Are You Now (7/91)
Wherever You Go (1/95)

GARTH BROOKS

Against the Grain (3/92)
Ain't Going Down (Til the Sun Comes Up) (8/93)
American Honky-Tonk Bar Association (9/93)
The Beaches of Cheyenne (12/95)
Callin' Baton Rouge (9/93)
The Dance (5/90)
Dixie Chicken (2/93)
The Fever (11/95)
Friends in Low Places (8/90)
Hard Luck Woman (7/94)
If Tomorrow Never Comes (9/89)
It's Midnight Cinderella (1/96)
Learning to Love Again (2/93)
Much Too Young
   (To Feel This Damn Old) (3/89)
Not Counting You (1/90)
The Old Man's Back in Town (12/92)
One Night a Day (9/93)
Papa Loved Mama (2/92)
The Red Strokes (11/94)
The River (5/92)
Rodeo (8/91)
Shameless (10/91)
She's Every Woman (8/95)
Somewhere Other Than the Night (10/92)
Standing Outside the Fire (9/93)
That Summer (5/93)
The Thunder Rolls (5/91)
Two of a Kind, Workin' on a Full House (2/91)
Unanswered Prayers (11/90)
We Shall Be Free (9/92)
What She's Doing Now (1/92)
White Christmas (12/94)

BROOKS & DUNN

Boot Scootin' Boogie (5/92)
Brand New Man (6/91)
Corine, Corina (3/94)
Hard Workin' Man (2/93)
I'll Never Forgive My Heart (11/94)
Little Miss Honky Tonk (2/95)
Lost and Found (9/92)
My Next Broken Heart (11/91)
Neon Moon (2/92)
Ride 'em High, Ride 'em Low (3/94)
Rock My World (Little Country Girl) (12/93)
She Used to Be Mine (9/93)
She's Not the Cheatin' Kind (8/94)
That Ain't No Way to Go (4/94)
We'll Burn That Bridge (5/93)
Whiskey Under the Bridge (9/95)
You're Gonna Miss Me When I'm Gone (6/95)

TRACY BYRD
The First Step (11/94)
Heaven in My Woman's Eyes (2/96)
Holdin' Heaven (6/93)
The Keeper of the Stars (1/95)
Lifestyles of the Not So Rich and Famous (4/94)
Love Lessons (8/95)
Someone to Give My Love To (2/93)
That's the Thing About a Memory (8/92)
Walking to Jerusalem (6/95)
Watermelon Crawl (8/94)
Why Don't That Telephone Ring (10/93)

KENNY CHESNEY
All I Need to Know (7/95)
Fall in Love (4/95)
Grandpa Told Me So (11/95)
The Tin Man (5/94)
Whatever It Takes (12/93)

MARK CHESNUTT
Almost Goodbye (9/93)
Blame It on Texas (3/91)
Broken Promise Land (10/91)
Brother Jukebox (11/90)
Bubba Shot the Jukebox (6/92)
Down in Tennessee (6/95)
Goin' Through the Big D (10/94)
Gonna Get a Life (2/95)
I Just Wanted You to Know (12/93)
I'll Think of Something (6/92)
It Wouldn't Hurt to Have Wings (12/95)
It Sure Is Monday (5/93)
Old Country (1/93)
Old Flames Have New Names (2/92)
She Dreams (7/94)
Too Cold at Home (8/90)
Trouble (9/95)
Woman, Sensuous Woman (4/94)
Your Love Is a Miracle (7/91)

MARK COLLIE
Born to Love You (1/93)
Calloused Hands (6/91)
Even the Man in the Moon Is Cryin' (8/92)
Hard Lovin' Woman (9/94)
Hardin County Line (10/90)
It Don't Take a Lot (3/92)
It Is No Secret (5/94)
Let Her Go (2/91)
Looks Aren't Everything (6/90)
Shame Shame Shame Shame (6/93)
She's Never Comin' Back (10/91)
Something's Gonna Change Her Mind (9/93)
Something with a Ring to It (2/90)
Three Words, Two Hearts, One Night (6/95)

BILLY RAY CYRUS
Achy Breaky Heart (Don't Tell My Heart) (4/92)
Could've Been Me (7/92)
Deja Blue (2/95)
In the Heart of a Woman (7/93)
She's Not Cryin' Anymore (9/92)
Some Gave All (6/92)
Somebody New (10/93)
Storm in the Heartland (10/94)
Talk Some (6/94)
Wher'm I Gonna Live? (10/92)
Words by Heart (1/94)

BILLY DEAN
Billy the Kid (5/92)
Cowboy Band (6/94)
I Wanna Take Care of You (4/93)
I'm Not Built That Way (8/93)
If There Hadn't Been You (8/92)
It's What I Do (2/96)
Men Will Be Boys (10/94)
Once in a While (3/94)
Only Here for a Little While (12/90)
Only the Wind (1/92)
Somewhere in My Broken Heart (5/91)
Tryin' to Hide a Fire in the Dark (12/92)
We Just Disagree (11/93)
You Don't Count the Cost (9/91)

DIAMOND RIO
Bubba Hyde (2/95)
Finish What We Started (5/95)
In a Week or Two (11/92)
Love a Little Stronger (5/94)
Mama Don't Forget to Pray for Me (11/91)
Meet in the Middle (3/91)
Mirror Mirror (7/91)
Night Is Fallin' in My Heart (10/94)
Norma Jean Riley (3/92)
Nowhere Bound (7/92)
Oh Me, Oh My, Sweet Baby (4/93)
Sawmill Road (11/93)
This Romeo Ain't Got Julie Yet (7/93)
Walkin' Away (8/95)

JOE DIFFIE
Bigger Than the Beatles (12/95)
Home (8/90)
Honky Tonk Attitude (3/93)
I'm in Love with a Capital "U" (5/95)
If the Devil Danced (In Empty Pockets) (4/91)
If You Want Me To (12/90)
In My Own Backyard (3/94)
Is It Cold in Here (12/91)
John Deere Green (11/93)

Leroy the Redneck Reindeer (12/95)
New Way (To Light Up an Old Flame) (8/91)
Next Thing Smokin' (8/92)
Not Too Much to Ask (with Mary-Chapin Carpenter) (9/92)
Pickup Man (10/94)
Prop Me Up Beside the Jukebox (If I Die) (7/93)
Ships That Don't Come (4/92)
So Help the Girl (2/95)
Startin' Over Blues (12/92)
That Road Not Taken (7/95)
Third Rock from the Sun (7/94)

FAITH HILL

But I Will (6/94)
It Matters to Me (11/95)
Let's Go to Vegas (8/95)
Piece of My Heart (2/94)
Take Me As I Am (9/94)
Wild One (10/93)

ALAN JACKSON

Blue Blooded Woman (10/89)
Chasin' That Neon Rainbow (10/90)
Chattahoochee (5/93)
Dallas (1/92)
Don't Rock the Jukebox (5/91)
Gone Country (8/94)
A Good Year for the Roses (with George Jones) (11/94)
Here in the Real World (1/90)
Honky Tonk Christmas (12/93)
I Don't Even Know Your Name (5/95)
I Only Want You For Christmas (12/91)
I'd Love You All Over Again (1/91)
I'll Try (12/95)
Livin' on Love (9/94)
Love's Got a Hold on You (7/92)
Mercury Blues (9/93)
Midnight in Montgomery (4/92)
She's Got the Rhythm (And I Got the Blues) (10/92)
Someday (8/91)
Song for the Life (2/95)
Summertime Blues (6/94)
Tall, Tall Trees (10/95)
Tequila Sunrise (10/93)
Tonight I Climbed the Wall (2/93)
Tropical Depression (8/93)
Wanted (6/90)
(Who Says) You Can't Have It All (1/94)

TOBY KEITH

Big Ol' Truck (7/95)
He Ain't Worth Missing (7/93)
A Little Less Talk and a Lot More Action (11/93)
Santa, I'm Right Here (12/95)
Should've Been a Cowboy (3/93)

Upstairs Downtown (12/94)
Who's That Man (7/94)
Wish I Didn't Know Now (3/94)
You Ain't Much Fun (3/95)

SAMMY KERSHAW

Anywhere But Here (10/92)
Cadillac Style (10/91)
Christmas Time's a Commin' (12/94)
Don't Go Near the Water (2/92)
Haunted Heart (5/93)
I Can't Reach Her Anymore (1/94)
If You're Gonna Walk, I'm Gonna Crawl (3/95)
National Working Woman's Holiday (5/94)
Never Bit a Bullet Like This (with George Jones) (3/94)
Queen of My Double Wide Trailer (9/93)
She Don't Know She's Beautiful (2/93)
Southbound (12/94)
Third Rate Romance (8/94)
Yard Sale (6/92)
Your Tattoo (7/95)

TRACY LAWRENCE

Alibis (2/93)
As Any Fool Can See (1/95)
Can't Break It to My Heart (6/93)
I See It Now (9/94)
If the Good Die Young (2/94)
If the World Had a Front Porch (7/95)
If You Loved Me (12/95)
My Second Home (9/93)
Renegades, Rebels and Rogues (5/94)
Runnin' Behind (6/92)
Somebody Paints the Wall (10/92)
Sticks and Stones (11/91)
Texas Tornado (4/95)
Today's Lonely Fool (2/92)

LITTLE TEXAS

Amy's Back in Austin (12/94)
Country Crazy (12/95)
First Time for Everything (2/92)
God Blessed Texas (7/93)
I'd Rather Miss You (1/93)
Kick a Little (8/94)
Life Goes On (8/95)
My Love (1/94)
Peaceful Easy Feeling (12/93)
Some Guys Have All the Love (9/91)
Southern Grace (4/95)
Stop on a Dime (5/94)
What Might Have Been (5/93)
What Were You Thinkin' (10/92)
You and Forever and Me (6/92)

THE MAVERICKS

All That Heaven Will Allow (5/95)
Here Comes the Rain (8/95)
Hey Good Lookin' (6/92)
I Should Have Been True (1/95)
O What a Thrill (5/94)
There Goes My Heart (10/94)
What a Cryin' Shame (1/94)

TERRY McBRIDE & THE RIDE

Been There (7/94)
Can I Count on You (3/91)
Going Out of My Mind (7/92)
High Hopes and Empty Pockets (11/94)
Hurry Sundown (7/93)
Just One Night (11/92)
Love on the Loose, Heart on the Run (3/93)
No More Cryin' (11/93)
Sacred Ground (3/92)
Same Old Star (8/91)
Somebody Will (2/95)

NEAL McCOY

The City Put the Country Back in Me (8/94)
For a Change (12/94)
If I Built You a Fire (1/91) 
If I Was a Drinkin' Man (8/95)
No Doubt About It (12/93)
Now I Pray for Rain (2/93)
There Ain't Nothin' I Don't Like About You (9/92)
They're Playing Our Song (4/92)
This Time I Hurt Her More (Than She Loves Me) (9/91)
Where Forever Begins (5/92)
You Gotta Love That (12/94)

TIM McGRAW

All I Want Is a Life (11/95)
Can't Really Be Gone (10/95)
Don't Take the Girl (4/94)
Down on the Farm (7/94)
I Like It, I Love It (8/95)
Indian Outlaw (1/94)
Memory Lane (4/93)
Not a Moment Too Soon (10/94)
Refried Dreams (2/95)
Two Steppin' Mind (7/93)
Welcome to the Club (10/92)

JOHN MICHAEL MONTGOMERY

Be My Baby Tonight (5/94)
Beer and Bones (7/93)
Cowboy Love (11/95)
I Can Love You Like That (2/95)
I Love the Way You Love Me (3/93)
I Swear (12/93)
If You've Got Love (9/94)
Kick It Up (4/94)
Life's a Dance (10/92)
No Man's Land (9/95)
Rope the Moon (3/94)
Sold (The Grundy County Auction Incident) (5/95)

COLLIN RAYE

All I Can Be (Is a Sweet Memory) (6/91)
Every Second (2/92) 
I Want You Bad (And That Ain't Good) (12/92)
If I Were You (4/95)
In This Life (8/92)
It Could've Been So Good (7/92)
Little Rock (4/94)
Love, Me (10/91)
Man of My Word (8/94)
My Kind of Girl (12/94)
Not That Different (11/95)
One Boy, One Girl (7/95)
Somebody Else's Moon (4/93)
That Was a River (8/93)
That's My Story (12/93)
What If Jesus Came Back Like That (11/95)

DOUG STONE

Addicted to a Dollar (2/94)
Born in the Dark (9/95)
Come in Out of the Pain (3/92)
Faith in Me, Faith in You (3/95)
Fourteen Minutes Old (7/90)
I Never Knew Love (10/93)
I Thought It Was You (7/91)
I'd Be Better Off (In a Pine Box) (3/90)
In a Different Light (3/91)
A Jukebox with a Country Song (11/91)
Made for Lovin' You (2/93)
More Love (6/94)
Little Houses (10/94)
Sometimes I Forget (5/95)
These Lips Don't Know How to Say Goodbye (11/90)
Too Busy Being in Love (11/92)
Warning Labels (7/92)
Why Didn't I Think of That (6/93)

DOUG SUPERNAW

Honky Tonkin' Fool (2/93)
I Don't Call Him Daddy (10/93)
Not Enough Hours in the Night (9/95)
Red and Rio Grande (2/94)
Reno (5/93)
State Fair (7/94)
What'll You Do About Me (1/95)
You Never Even Call Me By My Name (9/94)

AARON TIPPIN

The Call of the Wild (10/93)
Honky-Tonk Superman (2/94)
I Got It Honest (10/94)
I Was Born with a Broken Heart (10/92)
I Wonder How Far It Is Over You (4/91)
I Wouldn't Have It Any Other Way (6/92)
My Blue Angel (1/93)
She Feels Like a Brand New Man Tonight (2/95)
She Made a Memory Out of Me (8/91)
That's as Close as I'll Get to Loving You (8/95)
There Ain't Nothin' Wrong with the Radio (2/92)
Whole Lotta Love on the Line (4/94)
Without Your Love (2/96)
Working Man's Ph.D. (6/93)
You've Got to Stand for Something (11/90)

RICK TREVINO

Bobbie Ann Mason (5/95)
Doctor Time (10/94)
Honky Tonk Crowd (2/94)
Just Enough Rope (9/93)
Looking for the Light (2/95)
Save This One for Me (8/95)
She Can't Say I Didn't Cry (6/94)

TRAVIS TRITT

Anymore (9/91)
Between an Old Memory and Me (11/94)
Bible Belt (5/92)
Can I Trust You with My Heart (12/92)
Country Club (9/89)
Drift Off to Dream (2/91)
Foolish Pride (4/94)
Help Me Hold On (2/90)
Here's a Quarter (Call Someone
    Who Cares) (6/92)
I'm Gonna Be Somebody (6/90)
Looking Out for Number One (7/93)
Lord Have Mercy on the Working Man
    (Travis Tritt & Friends) (8/92)
Only You (And You Alone) (1/96)
Nothing Short of Dying (3/92)
Put Some Drive in Your Country (9/90)
Sometimes She Forgets (8/95)
Take It Easy (10/93)
Tell Me I Was Dreaming (4/95)
Ten Feet Tall and Bulletproof (8/94)
This One's Gonna Hurt You (For a Long, Long Time)
   (with Marty Stuart) (6/92)
T-R-O-U-B-L-E (12/92)

The Whiskey Ain't Workin' (with Marty Stuart) (11/91)
Worth Every Mile (10/93)

CLAY WALKER

Dreaming with My Eyes Open (6/94)
Hypnotize the Moon (1/96)
If I Could Make a Living (9/94)
Live Until I Die (10/93)
My Heart Will Never Know (5/95)
This Woman and This Man (1/95)
What's It to You (7/93)
Where Do I Fit in the Picture (2/94)
White Palace (4/94)
Who Needs You Baby (9/95)

TRISHA YEARWOOD

Better Your Heart Than Mine (2/94)
Down on My Knees (6/93)
I Fall to Pieces (with Aaron Neville) (6/94)
I Wanna Go Too Far (8/95)
It Wasn't His Child (12/94)
Like We Never Had a
    Broken Heart (9/91)
On a Bus to St. Cloud (12/95)
She's in Love with the Boy (5/91)
The Song Remembers When (10/93)
That's What I Like About You (12/91)
Walkaway Joe
    (with Don Henley) (11/92)
The Woman Before Me (3/92)
Wrong Side of Memphis (8/92)
XXX's and OOO's
    (An American Girl) (7/94)
You Can Sleep While I Drive (4/95)
You Say You Will (3/93)

ACHY BREAKY HEART
(DON'T TELL MY HEART)
Billy Ray Cyrus

Words and Music by
DON VON TRESS

Steady beat

You can tell the world you nev-er was my girl. You can burn my clothes when I'm gone. Or you can tell your friends just

You can tell your ma I moved to Ark-an-sas. You can tell your dog to bite my leg. Or tell your broth-er Cliff whose

Copyright © 1991 Millhouse Music
All Worldwide Rights Controlled by Songs Of PolyGram International, Inc.
International Copyright Secured   All Rights Reserved

what a fool I've been and laugh and joke about me on the
fist can tell my lip. He never really liked me any-

phone. Or You can tell my arms go
way. tell your Aunt Lou-ise. Tell

back to the farm. You can tell my feet to hit the
an-y-thing you please. My-self al-read-y knows I'm not o-

floor. Or you can tell my lips to
kay. Or you can tell my eyes to

tell my fin-ger-tips they won't be reach-ing out for you no
watch out for my mind. It might be walk-ing out on me to-

more.___
day.___ But Don't tell my heart, my

ach-y break-y heart.___ I just don't think he'd un-der-

stand. And if you tell my heart, my ach-y break-y heart,___ he might blow up and kill this man. Ooh.

Don't tell my heart, my ach-y break-y heart. I just don't think he'd under-stand. And if you tell my heart, my ach-y break-y heart, he might blow up and kill this man. Ooh.

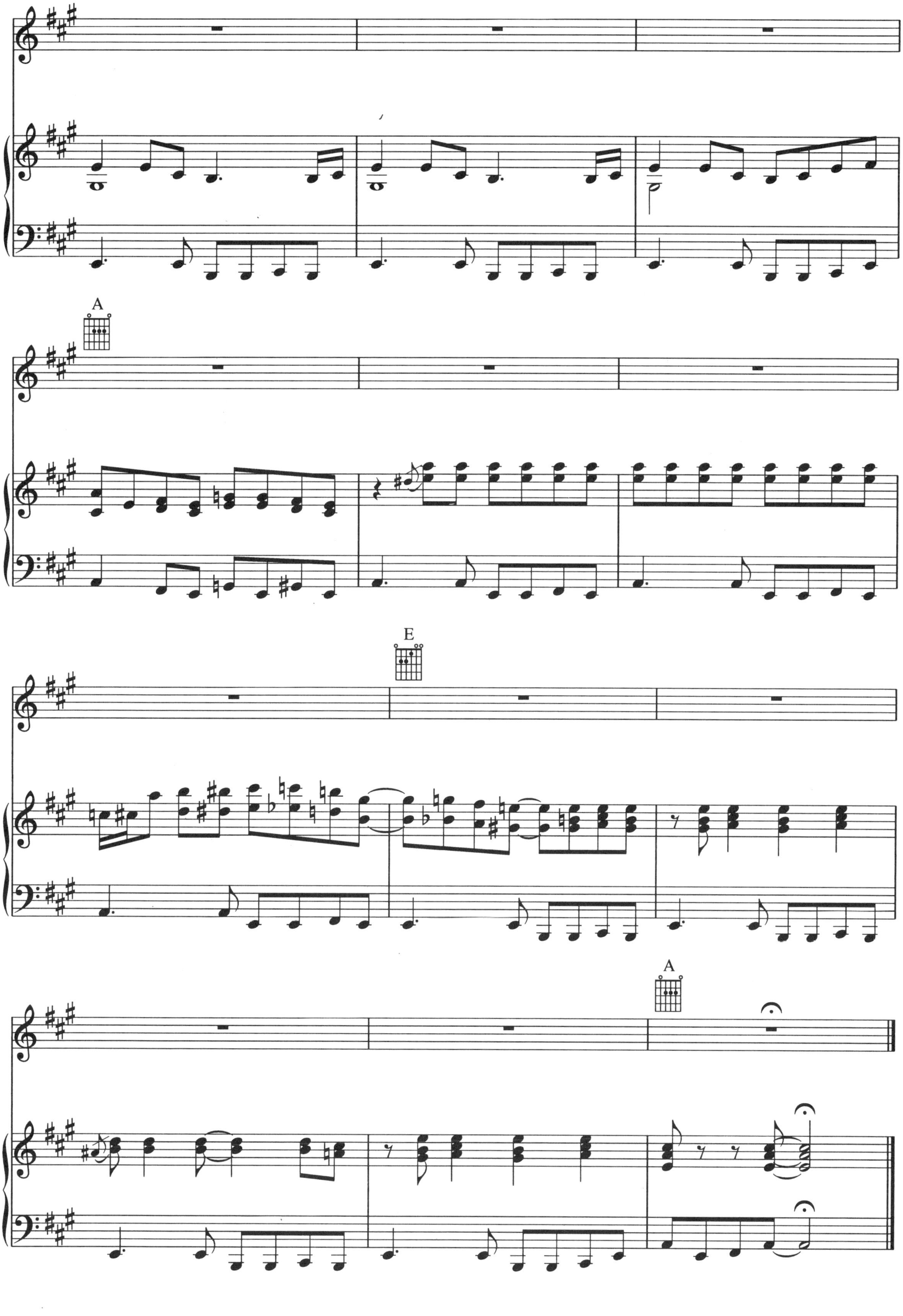
A
E
A

BOBBIE ANN MASON

Rick Trevino

Words and Music by
MARK D. SANDERS

Moderately

It was-n't the books that I did-n't read, it was-n't the teach-ers who tried to teach me. It was-n't that var-si-ty base-ball coach who kept on tell-in' them lock-er room jokes. It was

Bob-bie knew her his-t'ry, Bob-bie knew her French, Bob-bie knew how to keep a boy in sus-pense. She'd tease with a touch, she'd tease with a kiss. I was three long years be-in' teased by pret-ty Miss

Bob-bie grad-u-at-ed first in her class. Me, I grad-u-at-ed clos-er to last. Bob-bie went to col-lege, she got a de-gree. I got a gui-tar so I could sing a-bout me and

Copyright © 1995 Starstruck Writers Group, Inc. and Mark D. Music
International Copyright Secured   All Rights Reserved

Bob-bie Ann Ma-son back in high school; she was way too cute, she was way too cool. How was I gon-na get an ed-u-ca-tion sit-tin' right in back of Bob-bie Ann Ma-son?

Well,
Yeah,

18

- bie Ann Ma-son. *Instrumental solo - ad lib.*

Solo ends Well, the years have taught me the bas-ics of math: Di-vorce di-vides; time sub-tracts, takes a-way your hair, takes a-way your jump shot, but it ain't gon-na take all the

B
B
F#
mem-'ries I got of Bob-bie Ann Ma-son back in high school; she was
F#7
B
way too cute, she was way too cool.
How was I gon-na get an
F#
ed-u-ca-tion
1
F#7
sit-tin' right in back of
2
F#7
B
sit-tin' right in back of Bob-
F#7
B
bie Ann Ma-son, sit-tin' right in back of Bob-bie Ann Ma-son.

EVEN THE MAN IN THE MOON IS CRYIN'
Mark Collie

Words and Music by DON COOK
and MARK COLLIE

Moderate Country

walked her to the plane in Phoen - ix. I said, "Say hel - lo to your ma -
burn - in' up this black - top head - in' down to Aus -

ma." She could - n't e - ven look me in the eye.
tin. I won - der if she miss - es me to - night.

Copyright © 1991 Sony Tree Publishing Co., Inc., BMG Songs, Inc. and Judy Judy Judy Music
All Rights on behalf of Sony Tree Publishing Co., Inc. Administered by Sony Music Publishing, 8 Music Square West, Nashville, TN 37203
All Rights on behalf of Judy Judy Judy Music Administered by BMG Songs, Inc.
International Copyright Secured   All Rights Reserved

I drove out to the desert
I wish that I could tell her
just like nothin' happened and
how much I love her and I
somewhere in the darkness, I heard her say, "Good-bye."
Now, I hear voices in

the wind say-in' she ain't com-in' back a-gain. I look for guid-ance in the sky, but the stars have all gone out to-night. I feel like the love of my life is dy-in'. E-ven the man in the moon is cry-in'.

wish this damned old Thunder-bird could fly.

Now, I

I'm

Now, I hear voices in the wind sayin' she ain't comin' back again. I look for guidance in the sky, but the stars have all gone out tonight. I feel like the love of my life is dy - in'. E - ven the man in the moon is cry - in'.

E - ven the man in the moon

is cry - in.'

Repeat and Fade

FALL IN LOVE

Kenny Chesney

Words and Music by KIM WILLIAMS,
KENNY CHESNEY and BUDDY BROCK

Moderate Country

A lit-tle coun-try church on a two-lane road, a bride and a groom com-ing out the door. White
Old folks sit-ting in a front porch swing, still hold-ing hands like they were six-teen. Fif-

Copyright © 1995 Sony Cross Keys Publishing Co., Inc., Kim Williams Music and Acuff-Rose Music, Inc.
All Rights on behalf of Sony Cross Keys Publishing Co., Inc. and Kim Williams Music Administered by Sony Music Publishing, 8 Music Square West, Nashville, TN 37203
International Copyright Secured   All Rights Reserved

lace dress and a red bou-quet, "Just Mar-ried" writ-ten on a
ty good years they're a lov-er's dream. Dar - ling, that could be

blue Chev-ro-let. Don't that make you wan-na
you and me.

fall in love? Don't that look like a pic-ture of us? A match

made in heav-en if there ev-er was. Don't that make you wan-na fall? That just makes me wan-na give you my heart. Ev-'ry for-ev-er needs a place to start. Got-ta be a sign from up a-bove. Don't that make you wan-na fall in love?

Now, don't _ that make you wan-na fall in _ love? _

FOOLISH PRIDE
Travis Tritt

Words and Music by
TRAVIS TRITT

Moderately
no chord

She stayed up all night and cried
re- lives ev- 'ry word

in- to her pil- low,
they spoke in ang- er,

and fought off the urge to just break down and call.
He walks the floor and punch- es out the wall.

Copyright © 1994 Post Oak Publishing, Inc.
International Copyright Secured   All Rights Reserved

night to find the fault seemed so darned eas-y,
a-pol-o-gize to her would be so sim-ple,
but now, who's to blame don't mat-ter much at all.
but in-stead he cries, "I'll be damned if I'll crawl."

She thinks, if she calls him,
If he los-es her,

B♭
C
F
it just shows weak - ness.
So, the
he's lost his best friend
and
B♭
C
Dm
hurt goes on with ev - 'ry tear she's cried.
more than just a lov - er can pro - vide.
C
B♭
Ain't it sad to see a good love fall to piec -
So, he wrest - les with e - mo - tions that de - feat
F
B♭
F
- es?
him.
Chalk an - oth - er heart break up
Chalk an - oth - er love lost up

to fool-ish pride.
to fool-ish pride. Turn out the
lights, the com-pe-ti-tion's o-ver.
The stub-born souls are the los-ers here to-night.
And while the bri-dges burn

an - oth - er hard, hard les - son's learned as in the ash - es pas - sion slow - ly dies. And this ro - mance goes down to fool - ish pride, yeah.

35

FRIENDS IN LOW PLACES

Garth Brooks

Words and Music by DEWAYNE BLACKWELL
and EARL BUD LEE

last one to show;__ I was the last__ one you thought you'd see there.__ And I saw the sur-prise__ and the fear in his eyes__ when I took his glass__ of cham-pagne and I toast-ed you,__ said, "Hon-ey,

just say good-night__ and I'll show__ my-self__ to the door.__ Hey, I did-n't mean__ to cause a big scene__ just give me an ho-ur and then,__ well I'll be as high__ as that i-

we may be through_ but you'll nev - er hear__ me com - plain."_
- vo - ry tow - er that you're liv - in' in. ___
A
'Cause I've got friends_ in low plac - es where the
whis - key___ drowns_ and the beer___ chas - es my blues_
Bm7
E
___ a - way and I'll be o - kay.______

39

Bm7
E
A
D.S. al Coda
Well, I
CODA
I've got friends_ in low plac - es where the
whis - key___ drowns_ and the beer___ chas - es my blues_

a - way and I'll be o - kay.

Yeah, I'm not big on so - cial grac - es. Think I'll slip on down to the o - a - sis. Oh, I've got friends in low plac - es.

Repeat and Fade

GONE COUNTRY
Alan Jackson

Words and Music by
BOB McDILL

Moderately

She's been play-ing that room on the strip for ten years in Ve-gas.
folk scene's dead, but he's hold-ing out in the vil-lage.
mutes to L. A., but he's got a house in the Val-ley.

Ev-'ry night she looks in the mir-ror, and she on-ly
He's been writ-ing songs, speak-ing out a-gainst wealth and
But the bills are pil-ing up, and the pop scene just ain't gon-na

Copyright © 1994 PolyGram International Publishing, Inc. and Ranger Bob Music
International Copyright Secured All Rights Reserved

ag - es. She's been
priv - ilege. He says,
ral - ly. He says,

read - in' 'bout Nash - ville and all the rec - ords that ev - 'ry - bod - y's
"I don't be - lieve in mon - ey, but a man could make him a
"Hon - ey, I'm a se - ri - ous com - pos - er, schooled in voice and com - po -

buy - ing. Says, "I'm a
kill - in', 'cause
si - tion, but with the

sim - ple girl my - self; grew up on Long Is - land."
some of that stuff don't sound much dif - f'rent than Dyl - an.
crime and the smog these days L. A.'s no place for chil - dren.

So, she packs her bags to try her hand. Says,
I hear down there it's changed, you see. They're
Lord, it sounds so eas-y. It should-n't take long. Be

"This might be my last chance." She's gone coun-try.
not as back-ward as they used to be." He's gone coun-try.
back in the mon-ey in no time at all." He's gone coun-try.

Look at them boots. She's gone coun-try,
Look at them boots. He's gone coun-try,
Look at them boots. He's gone coun-try,

back to her roots. She's gone coun-try, a
back to his roots. He's gone coun-try, a
back to his roots. He's gone coun-try, a

new kind of suit. She's gone coun-try.
new kind of suit. He's gone coun-try.
new kind of suit. He's gone coun-try.

(Spoken:) Here she comes!

Well, the

(Spoken:) Here he comes!

D.S. al Coda
He com -
CODA
G
(Spoken:) Here he comes!
D
C
G
D
C
Yeah, he's gone
G
C
D
coun - try,
a new kind of walk.
gonna make his move.
He's gone
G
C
D
Repeat ad lib. and Fade
coun - try,
a new kind of talk.
back to his roots.
He's gone

I CAN LOVE YOU LIKE THAT

John Michael Montgomery

Words and Music by STEVE DIAMOND,
MARIBETH DERRY and JENNIFER KIMBALL

Moderate Ballad

With pedal

They read you Cin-der-el-la, you hoped it would come true that one day your Prince Charm-ing would come res-cue you. You

nev-er make a prom-ise I don't in-tend to keep. So, when I say for-ev-er, for-ev-er's what I mean.

© 1995 Diamond Cuts, Criterion Music Corp., Full Keel Music Co., Second Wave Music and Friends And Angels Music
All Rights for Diamond Cuts in the U.S. and Canada Administered by Seven Summits Music
All Rights for Second Wave Music and Friends And Angels Music Administered by Full Keel Music Co.
International Copyright Secured All Rights Reserved

C
Em
like ro - man - tic mov - ies; you nev - er will __ for - get the
I'm no Ca - sa - no - va, but I swear this much is true:
F
G7sus
Em7
way you felt when Ro - me - o kissed Ju - li - et. __ All this time that you've been wait -
I'll be hold - ing noth - ing back when it comes to you. You dream of love that's ev - er - last -
F
Em7
F
- ing, you don't have to wait no ______ more.
- ing. Well, ba - by, o - pen up your ______ eyes.
G7sus
C
Em
I can love you like that. I would make you my world, _ move heav - en and earth _

49

2
C
Gm7
3 fr
You want ten - der - ness, I got ten -
Dm7
C
- der - ness. And I see through _ to the
Gm7
3 fr
Dm7
heart of you. _ If you want a man who un - der - stands, _
F
G7sus
you don't have to look ver - y far. _

G
C
I can love you, I can, I can love you like that.
I would make you my world,
Em
F
move heav - en and earth if you were my girl.
G7sus
C
Em
I will give you my heart, be all that you need, show you you're ev -
Repeat and Fade
F
G7sus
- 'ry - thing that's precious to me. I can love you like that.

I WANNA GO TOO FAR

Trisha Yearwood

Words and Music by LAYNG MARTINE, JR.
and KENT ROBBINS

Moderately

Ev-'ry-thing in mod-er-a-tion, that's the way it's al-ways been. Nev-er get-tin' out of con-trol,
I'm the one they all de-pend on, sen-si-ble, pre-dict--a-ble and strong. But ev-'ry now and then

Copyright © 1995 by Careers-BMG Music Publishing, Inc., Doo Layng Songs, Irving Music, Inc. and Colter Bay Music
All Rights for Doo Layng Songs Administered by Careers-BMG Music Publishing, Inc.
International Copyright Secured   All Rights Reserved

[Am] nev-er hang-in' it out, [G] al-ways reel-in' it in. [F] I saved my
I feel like I played that role too long. I need to rock the

[G] mon-ey for a rain-y day, [F/A] but now I've had e-nough [G/B] of play-in' it safe.
boat, I need to speak my mind. Just this once __ let it all un-wind.

[C] 1,2. I wan-na go too far, __ [F] I wan-na go __ too fast. __
D.S. *Instrumental solo*

[G] __ [C] Some-bod-y draw the line __

54

(Solo ends) so I can blow right past. I wan-na spend too much, I wan-na stay too late, I'm gon-na roar too loud, I'm gon-na be that way. I wan-na play too hard, I wan-na go too

far.

I've got-ta set this spir-it free, it's hid-ing here in-side. I feel like a bird in a cage, time for me to fly, _____ yeah, _____ yeah. _____

CODA

Yeah, I wan-na go _____ too far. _____

Yeah, _____ I wan-na go _____ too

far.

IF THE DEVIL DANCED
(IN EMPTY POCKETS)
Joe Diffie

Words and Music by KIM WILLIAMS
and KEN SPOONER

Moderate country two-beat (♪♪ played as ♪₃♪)

Instrumental solo

-blo mo-tors had a hell of a sale, _____ down-
He said friend it ain't _____ the end _____ let's see _____

-town yes-ter-day, _____ Word _____
what I can do. _____ If you

Copyright © 1989 Sony Cross Keys Publishing Co., Inc. and Texas Wedge Music
All Rights on behalf of Sony Cross Keys Publishing Co., Inc. Administered by Sony Music Publishing, 8 Music Square West, Nashville, TN 37203
International Copyright Secured   All Rights Reserved

C7

got a - round, no mon - ey down, take
own a home, I've got a loan,

A7 **D**

years and years to pay. When I
tai - lor made for you. Then a -

C7

got there, the lot was bare, but the
bove the rack - et a voice in my jack - et said,

G **C7** **C#dim**

sales - man said hold on. For a lit - tle cash, I got ta
"I'll tote the note." The de - vil made me do it, talked

two-tone Nash out behind the barn.
me into it, and that was all she wrote.

Solo ends If the devil danced in empty pockets, he'd have a ball in mine. With a nine foot grand, a ten piece band and a twelve girl chorus line. I'd raise

_____ some loot _____ in a three piece suit, give 'em one dance_____ for a dime._____

If the de - vil danced in emp - ty pock - ets,

he'd have a ball_____ in mine._____ Well

They say debt is a bot - tom - less pit where the de - vil likes to play._____

I'd sell my soul to get out of this hole, but there'd be hell to pay.

D.S. al Coda

If There Hadn't Been You

Billy Dean

Words and Music by RON HELLARD
and TOM SHAPIRO

Moderate Country Ballad

A man filled with doubt, down and out and so a-lone, a ship tossed and turned, lost and yearn-ing for a home,

A man filled with hope who fin-'ly knows where he be-longs, a heart filled with love, more than e-nough to keep it strong,

Copyright © 1992 by Careers-BMG Music Publishing, Inc., Edge O' Woods Music, Kinetic Diamond Music and Moline Valley Music
International Copyright Secured All Rights Reserved

a sur-vi-vor bare-ly sur-viv - ing, not real-ly sure of his next move, all of this I would have been if there had-n't been you.

a life that's a-live a-gain, no long-er a-fraid to face the truth, all of this I would have missed if there had-n't been you.

If there had-n't been you,

A♭
B♭
where would I be if there had - n't been you
E♭
A♭
E♭
Cm
here for me? I made it through times I
Gm7
A♭(add9)
Fm7
nev - er would have made it through
1
B♭
E♭
if there had - n't been you.

B♭6
A♭maj7
A♭(add9)
A
2
B♭
E♭/G
A♭
B♭
Cm
B♭/D
if there had-n't been you on my side,
E♭
E♭/G
A♭
A♭m6
E♭
you in my life. All my dreams would still be dreams
B♭
E♭
Cm
if there had-n't been you.

All_ my_ dreams_ would still be dreams_ if there had-n't been_ you.

IF YOU'RE GONNA WALK, I'M GONNA CRAWL

Sammy Kershaw

Words and Music by BUDDY CANNON
and LARRY BASTIAN

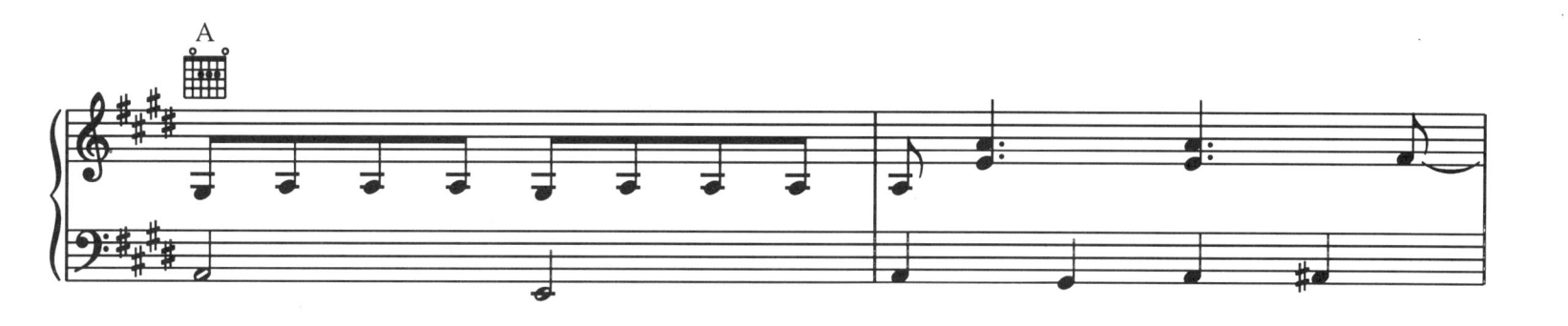

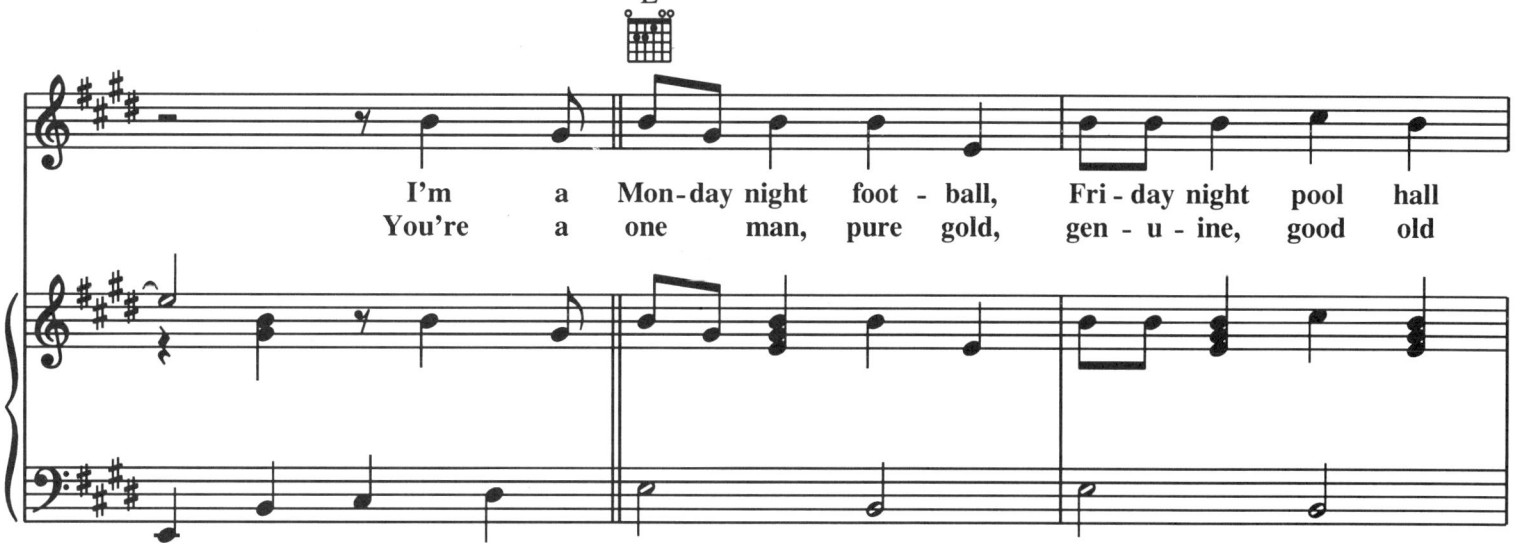

Moderately fast

I'm a Mon-day night foot-ball, Fri-day night pool hall
You're a one man, pure gold, gen-u-ine, good old

Copyright © 1994 Songs Of PolyGram International, Inc., Hotdoggone Music and Buttonwillow Music
International Copyright Secured   All Rights Reserved

guy.____ I ain't nev-er been one to let a
girl.____ You've been wait-in' on me to get

good time pass me by.____ You're stand-
tired of my ne-on world.____ Now the

-in' there stat-in' you're tired____ of wait-in'; our
turn you've tak-in' has got____ me shak-en, it's a

cel-e-brat-in's grat-in' on____ you.____ If you
heart-break-in' wake-up____ call.____

feel that way ___ if it-'ll make you stay, ___ well here's ___
Now I'm see - in' how ___ you see me ___ and I

___ what I'm gon-na do. ___
feel 'bout a shoe top tall. ___

If you're gon-na walk, _____ I'm ___ gon-na crawl.

You'll see how low ___ a man ___

can go when his back's _a-gainst_ the wall._ I'll be grov-el-in' in the grav-el _____ if you make_ that tax-i call._ If you're gon-na walk, _ I'm _ gon-na crawl. _____ crawl. _____

71

IN A WEEK OR TWO

Diamond Rio

Words and Music by GARY BURR
and JAMES HOUSE

Easy Country Ballad

In a week or two
A little more time

I would have been ready.
was all I needed,

I would have known what to say,
but somehow fall became spring.

© Copyright 1992 by MCA MUSIC PUBLISHING, A Division of MCA INC., GARY BURR MUSIC, INC., SONY TREE PUBLISHING CO., INC. and MAD WOMEN MUSIC
All Rights for GARY BURR MUSIC, INC. Controlled and Administered by MCA MUSIC PUBLISHING, A Division of MCA INC.
All Rights for SONY TREE PUBLISHING CO., INC. and MAD WOMEN MUSIC Administered by SONY MUSIC PUBLISHING, 8 Music Square West, Nashville, TN 37203
International Copyright Secured   All Rights Reserved

MCA music publishing

but I missed my chance
You put off to-day
when the words "I love you" came just a lit-tle too late.
what you can do to-mor-row. Well, some-times it don't do a thing.

In a week or two I was gon-na bring you dia-monds. In a week or two, a long, long string of pearls. And we would have run down to the riv-er at night, sailed a-way just me and you in a week or two.

two. These words in my heart never had a

75

THE KEEPER OF THE STARS
Tracy Byrd

Words and Music by DICKEY LEE,
DANNY MAYO and KAREN STALEY

Moderately slow

It was no ac-ci-dent,_ me find-ing you.
Soft moon-light on your face,_ oh, how_ you shine.

Some-one_ had a hand in it_
It takes_ my_ breath a-way_

Copyright © 1994 Songs Of PolyGram International, Inc., Pal Time Music, Sixteen Stars Music, New Haven Music, Inc. and Murrah Music Corp.
International Copyright Secured   All Rights Reserved

long be-fore__ we ev-er knew.   Now I____ just
just to look__ in-to your eyes.   I know__ I

can't__ be-lieve__   you're in__ my
don't__ de-serve__   a treas-ure__ like

life.   Heav-en's smil-in'
you.   There real-ly____

down on me____ as I look at you__ to-
are no words__ to show my grat-i-

night.
tude.

So, I tip my hat
So, I tip my hat to the Keeper of the Stars. He sure knew what he was doin' when he joined these two hearts. I hold ev - 'ry -

thing when I hold ___ you in my arms. I've got all ___ I'll ev - er need, thanks to the Keep - er of ___ the Stars. Stars. Stars.

A/C♯
It was _ no ac - ci - dent, _
Bm
G
me find - ing you.
D/F♯
Some - one had a hand in it _
Em
A7
D
A7sus
D
long be - fore _ we ev - er knew.
rit.

LIFE GOES ON
Little Texas

Words and Music by KEITH FOLLESE,
DEL GRAY and THOM McHUGH

The sun comes up, the sun goes down, this old world keeps spinnin' a-round. Not much has changed since you've been gone. I miss you, hon-ey, but life goes on.

You

Copyright © 1995 by Careers-BMG Music Publishing, Inc., Breaker Maker Music, Howlin' Hits Music, Inc., Square West Music, Inc., Kicking Bird Music, Inc. and Thomahawk Music
All Rights for Breaker Maker Music Administered by Careers-BMG Music Publishing, Inc.
All Rights for Thomahawk Music Administered by Kicking Bird Music, Inc.
International Copyright Secured   All Rights Reserved

It's nice to see you still think a-bout me, but don't wor-ry a-bout my heart.
say you can tell that I'm do-in' well by the sound of my voice.

Thanks for the call. Yeah, I took a fall, but
What'd you ex-pect? Ba-by, when you left,

I did-n't fall a-part. The sun comes up, the
you left me no choice.

sun goes down, this old world keeps spin-nin' a-round.

Not much has changed since you've been gone. ____ I miss you, hon-ey, but life ____ goes on. ____ goes on. ____

Thanks to you say-in' we're through I've got-ten good at get-tin' by.

I don't know when, but I'll love a-gain.

It's just a mat-ter of time. The sun comes up, the sun goes down, this old world keeps spin-nin' a-round. Not much has changed since you've been gone. I miss you, hon-ey, but life goes on.

I miss you, hon-ey, but life goes on. I miss you, hon-ey, but life

goes on.

LET'S GO TO VEGAS
Faith Hill

Words and Music by
KAREN STALEY

Moderately fast

Lyin' on the bank of the river, stars ___ are dancin', Lord, ___ it's hot. Holdin' you is what I live for. I ___ just had a crazy thought. ___ Hey, baby, let's

We'll find ___ a little wedding ___ chapel, a pair of rings and a preacher, too. Underneath the neon steeple we'll take a gamble and say, "I do." ___

Copyright © 1993 Sony Tree Publishing Co., Inc. and All Over Town Music
All Rights Administered by Sony Music Publishing, 8 Music Square West, Nashville, TN 37203
International Copyright Secured   All Rights Reserved

go to Ve - gas, kiss the sin - gle life good - bye. _____ Hey, ba - by, let's

go to Ve - gas, bet on love __ and let it ride.

Vi - va, Las __ Ve - gas,

sparkl-in' lights, dan-ger-ous liv-in', tum-bl-in' dice. You're my ace in the hole now, hon-ey, I'm your la-dy luck. Pack a few things and a lit-tle mon-ey and put 'em in the truck. Hey, ba-by, let's go to Ve-gas, kiss the sin-gle life good-bye. _____ Hey, ba-by, let's go to Ve- gas, bet on love _ and let it ride.

CODA
C
G
let it ride. Hey, ba - by, let's go to Ve - gas,
D
G
kiss the sin - gle life good - bye. Hey, ba - by, let's
C
D
C
G
go to Ve - gas, bet on love and let it ride,
C
D
C
G
bet on love and let it ride,

91

bet on love ___ and let it ride. ___

MY HEART WILL NEVER KNOW

Clay Walker

Words and Music by STEVE DORFF
and BILLY KIRSCH

Moderate ballad

I pour two cups of cof-fee, put the
It's been a long,___ cold De-cem - ber; the

pa - per on___ the ta - ble so we can share___ the morn-ing
snow out - side___ keeps fall - ing. I'll light a fire___ when you get

Copyright © 1994 by Galewood Songs, Ensign Music Corporation, Issy Moon Music and Kidbilly Music
International Copyright Secured   All Rights Reserved

93

news. / home.
Your voice answers our phone / It reminds me of the first

when we're not home. Friends who call can leave a
night we made love like it would last forever and

message here for you. Ev'ry night
nothing could go wrong. You're a part

I leave the light on; you're just working late.
of me, a part of ev'rything I do.

As far as I can see, ev-'ry-thing is still the same.
I keep hold-ing on, hid-ing from the truth.

And my } heart will nev-er know, so I don't fall a-part.
So, my

I fool my-self for an-oth-er day, and

you're not real-ly gone. After all this time,

it's still too hard to let you go. As long as I don't say good-bye, my heart will never know.

know.

After all __ this time, __ it's still too hard to let you go. __ As long as I don't say good-bye, my heart will nev-er know. __

NO DOUBT ABOUT IT

Neal McCoy

Words and Music by JOHN SCOTT SHERRILL
and STEVE SESKIN

In a moderate 2

mf

Just __ like ev - 'ry lock's got __ to have a
nail, socks __ and
lock's got __ to have a

key, ev - 'ry riv - er goes look - in' for the
shoes, we __ go hand in hand like rhy - thm and __
key, ev - 'ry riv - er goes look - in' for the

Copyright © 1993 Sony Tree Publishing Co., Inc., All Over Town Music, New Wolf Music and Love This Town Music
All Rights on behalf of Sony Tree Publishing Co., Inc., All Over Town Music and New Wolf Music Administered by Sony Music Publishing, 8 Music Square West, Nashville, TN 37203
International Copyright Secured   All Rights Reserved

sea. And when you plant a seed, it reaches for the
blues. What good is a man if he hasn't got a
sea. And when you plant a seed, it reaches for the

sky. That's just the way it is, nobody wonders
dream? 'Bout as good as a car with no gasoline.
sky. That's just the way it is, girl, with you and

why. Like coffee needs a cup, you know that it ain't
You're the one I'm dreamin' of. Got to have your
I. Like coffee needs a cup, you know that it ain't

much good without it.
love; I can't live without it.
much good without it.

We were meant to be to-geth-er, no doubt a-bout it.

Oh, there ain't no doubt a-bout it.

To Coda

Like a ham-mer and a   *Some-thing was miss-ing; it was mak-ing me blue.*   *But all I ev-er need-ed was you.*   *Just like ev-'ry*

D.S. al Coda

CODA

101

ONE BOY, ONE GIRL

Collin Raye

Words and Music by MARK ALAN SPRINGER
and SHAYE SMITH

Tenderly

He fin-'lly gave in __ to his friend's __ girl - friend __ when she said, __ "There's some - one __ you should meet." __ At a crowd - ed res - t'rant way __ cross town __ he wait - ed im - pa - tient - ly. __

no time at all __ they were stand - ing there __ in the front __ of a lit - tle __ church, __ a - mong their friends __ and fam - i - ly, __ re - peat - ing those sa - cred words. __

© 1995 EMI Blackwood Music Inc. and Mark Alan Springer Music
All Rights Controlled and Administered by EMI Blackwood Music Inc.
All Rights Reserved   International Copyright Secured   Used by Permission

when she walked in, ____ their eyes met ____
The preach-er said, ____ "Son, kiss your bride," ____
and they both stared. ____ And right there and then ____ ev-
and he raised her veil. Like the night they met, ____ time ____

-'ry-one else ____ dis-ap-peared ____ but } one boy, ____
just ____ stood ____ still ____ for

one girl, ____ two hearts beat-ing wild-

-ly. To put it mild-ly, it was love at first sight. He smiled, she smiled, and they knew right a-way this was the day they'd wait-ed for all their lives.

For a moment the whole world revolved around one boy and one girl.

To Coda

In

He was holding her hand when the doc-

-tor looked up ____ and grinned. _____

"Con - grat - u - la - tions! _____

Twins." One boy, ____

rit.

REFRIED DREAMS

Tim McGraw

Words and Music by JIM FOSTER
and MARK PETERSEN

I head-ed south out of Del Ri-o, Tex-as, one
Shoot-in' te-qui-la, want-ing to kill ya and

hell of a load on my brain. And I kept on go-ing with-
wish-in' to God you were near. So full of your mem-'ry but

out e-ven know-ing how much your love real-ly means.
feel-ing so emp-ty, I've run out of my self-es-teem.

Now I'm messed up in Mex-i-co,

livin' on re-fried dreams.

I'm down here in Mexico, sick as a dog. My head is poundin' in this border town fog. Down to my last dime and coming apart at the seams,

Em
C
D
G
I'm messed up in Mex - i - co,
D
To Coda
1 G
D
liv - in' on re - fried dreams.
G
D
This
2 G
D.S. al Coda
dreams.
I'm

dreams. Oh, I'm messed up in Mexico, livin' on refried dreams.

SACRED GROUND

McBride & The Ride

Words and Music by KIX BROOKS
and VERNON RUST

Moderately

We got mar-ried in high-school, had a ba-by when we turned eight-een.
guess I took for grant-ed she would nev-er look at some-one else. Now

I bagged gro-ceries in the day-time. At night
I got some patch-ing up to do. Oh, and

Copyright © 1987 Sony Cross Keys Publishing Co., Inc., Fort Kix Music and David 'N' Will Music
All Rights on behalf of Sony Cross Keys Publishing Co., Inc. and Fort Kix Music Administered by Sony Music Publishing, 8 Music Square West, Nashville, TN 37203
International Copyright Secured All Rights Reserved

113

take her with-out a fight.
took so long to build.

This ain't just some ne-on love come late-ly. It's a pre-cious thing you don't know noth-ing a-bout.

We were joined in the eyes of the Lord, in the eyes of our hometown. Why don't you leave her alone? You're treading on sacred ground.

2.
G
Em7
Am
Go on and leave her a - lone.
G/B
C
D
Why don't you leave her a - lone?
Go on and
Am
G/B
C
D
leave her a - lone.
You're tread-ing on sa - cred ground.
C6/9
G
rit.

STANDING ON THE EDGE OF GOODBYE

John Berry

Words and Music by STEWART HARRIS
and JOHN BERRY

Moderately

It's been a long time since I've held her close. And we've misplaced feelings that we used to know.

All of those years came rushing through my mind, and I found myself back in a simpler time.

Copyright © 1995 Sony Tree Publishing Co., Inc., Edisto Sound International and Kicking Bird Music, Inc.
All Rights on behalf of Sony Tree Publishing Co., Inc. and Edisto Sound International Administered by Sony Music Publishing, 8 Music Square West, Nashville, TN 37203
International Copyright Secured   All Rights Reserved

| Gm | F | E♭ |

Thought I could see between the lines I read,
Just two young kids runnin' on fire and dreams.

| Cm | B♭/D | E♭ |

but I wasn't ready when she turned to me and said,
And in her eyes I realized she was calling out to me.

| Fsus | F | E♭ |

She said, "I can't eat and I can't sleep.

| B♭ | E♭ | B♭ |

Sometimes I find it hard to breathe. I break down and

Cm7
3fr
B♭/D
E♭
3fr
cry not know-ing why. But now I can't lie, I'm
F
E♭
3fr
1
stand-ing on the edge of good - bye."
Fsus
2
Fsus
Good - bye.
F
Gm
3fr
I would do an - y-thing to

E♭
Cm
3fr
let her know there's just no way
B♭/D
E♭
Cm7
Fsus
my heart can let her go.
F
E♭
B♭
'Cause I can't eat and I can't sleep. Some-times I find
E♭
B♭
Cm7
it hard to breathe. I break down and cry not know-ing
3

B♭/D
E♭
3fr
F
why. But now I can't lie, she's stand-ing on the edge of good -
E♭
3fr
Fsus
bye. Good - bye.
1 F
2 F
B♭
And I can't eat Stand-ing on the edge of good - bye.
E♭
3fr
Repeat and Fade
Stand-ing on the edge of good -

SHE DREAMS
Mark Chesnutt

Words and Music by TIM MENSY
and GARY HARRISON

In a flowing motion

Thir-ty years to-day she's been up-on this earth and
he's proud of his work and the lad-der that he's climbed, but

---

Copyright © 1991 Sony Cross Keys Publishing Co., Inc., Miss Dot Music, Inc., Brass Ring Music, Warner-Tamerlane Publishing Corp. and Patrick Joseph Music, Inc.
All Rights on behalf of Sony Cross Keys Publishing Co., Inc., Miss Dot Music, Inc. and Brass Ring Music Administered by Sony Music Publishing, 8 Music Square West, Nashville, TN 37203
All Rights on behalf of Patrick Joseph Music, Inc. Administered by Warner-Tamerlane Publishing Corp.
International Copyright Secured   All Rights Reserved

[D7sus] she can't help but won-der what it's all
[D7] from that high rise of-fice he can't hear

[G] [C/G] been worth.
her cry.
[G] She

[D7sus] swears she loves those kids and she
Ring-ing tel-e-phones, de-

[D7]

[D7sus] does-n't mind that load, but there
ci-sions to be made, and

[D7]

ain't much con-ver-sa-tion with a three-year-old.
e-ven when he gets home, he's still far a-way.

She's trapped in-side these walls, a
Then he drifts off to sleep and

pris-oner in this fine sub-ur-ban home.
she en-ters her world of make be-lieve.

So, she dreams,
And, she dreams,
she dreams

he'll come home ____ from work ____ and car-ry her ____ a - way. ____ And he'll see ____ she needs ____ the man ____ she's still in love ____ with when ____ she dreams. ____

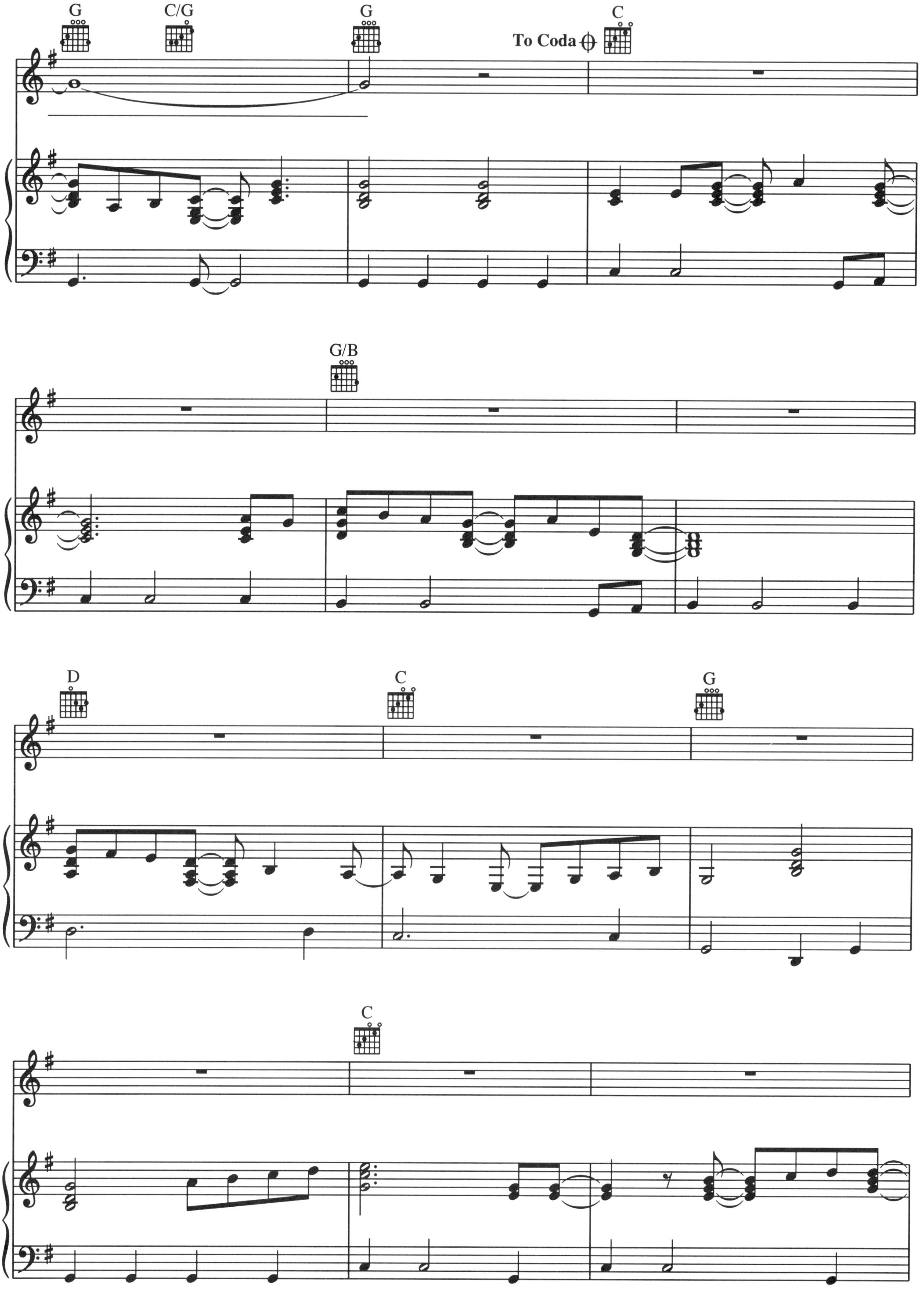
G
C/G
G
To Coda
C
G/B
D
C
G
C

127

THAT AIN'T MY TRUCK
Rhett Akins

Words and Music by RHETT AKINS,
CHRIS WATERS and TOM SHAPIRO

Copyright © 1994 Sony Tree Publishing Co., Inc., Great Cumberland Music and Diamond Struck Music
All Rights on behalf of Sony Tree Publishing Co., Inc. Administered by Sony Music Publishing, 8 Music Square West, Nashville, TN 37203
International Copyright Secured   All Rights Reserved

Said she'd let us know by to-night which one it would be. So I waited by the phone, but she never called me up. Had to know what was go-in' on, so I drove by her house, and sure enough

won-d'rin' what it was I did so wrong that he did so right. I thought of break-in' down the door, but there's nothin' left to say. That Chev-y four-by-four says it all, sit-tin' in my place.

that ain't my truck in her drive. Man, this ain't my day tonight. Looks like she's in love and I'm out of luck. That ain't my shadow on her wall. Lord, this don't look good at all. That's my girl, my whole world, but that ain't my truck.

I pulled truck.

That ain't my shadow on her wall. Lord, this don't look good at all. That's my girl, my whole world, but that ain't my truck.

133

There Goes My Heart

The Mavericks

Words and Music by RAUL MALO
and KOSTAS

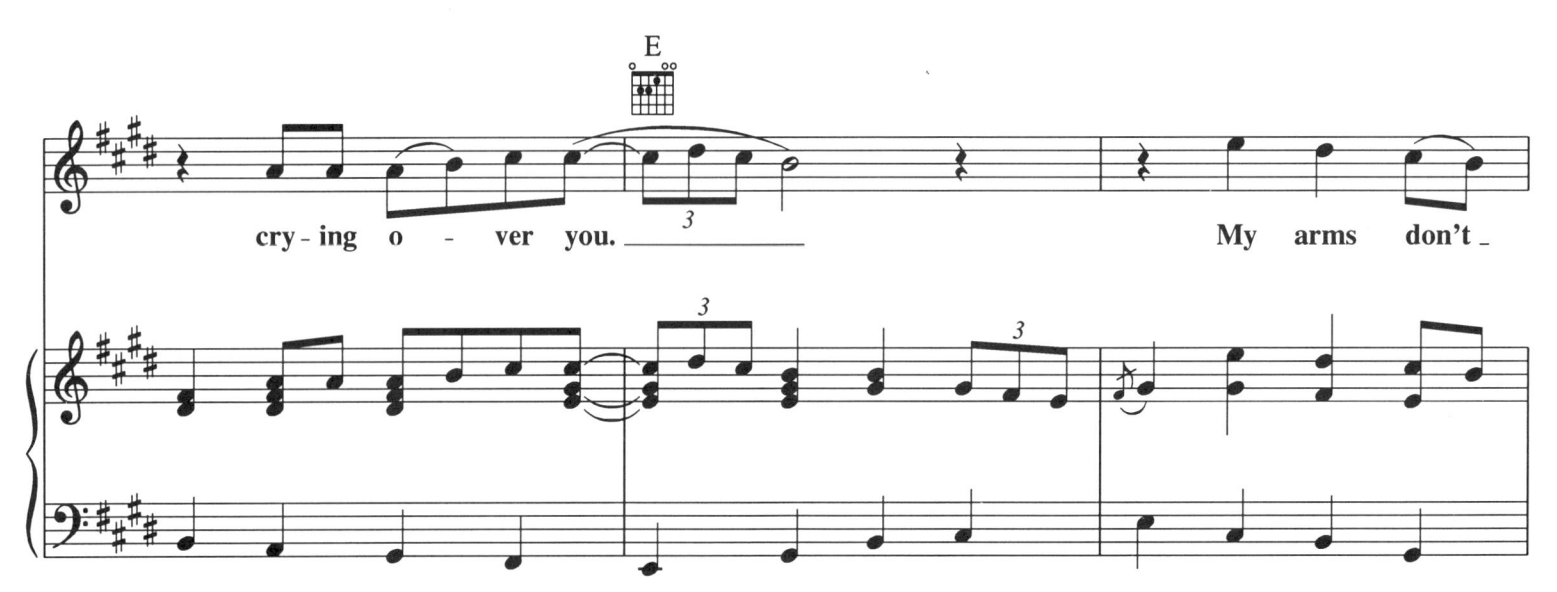

Country shuffle

There goes my heart breaking in two.

There go my eyes crying over you. My arms don't

Copyright © 1994 Sony Tree Publishing Co., Inc., Raul Malo Music, Songs Of PolyGram International, Inc. and Seven Angels Music
All Rights on behalf of Sony Tree Publishing Co., Inc. and Raul Malo Music Administered by Sony Music Publishing, 8 Music Square West, Nashville, TN 37203
International Copyright Secured   All Rights Reserved

want ___ for us ___ to part.

So, when you go, ___ here come the blues, ___ there goes my heart. ___

You told me ___ once ___ we'd ___ nev - er
on ___ a bridge ___ that's

part ___ that you loved ___ me ___
burned. ___ It's just a ___ lone -

_____ with all _____ your heart. _____ But now these
- ly _____ les - son learned. To see you

words of love _____ you're go - ing _____ to e - rase. _____
walk a - way _____ with him _____ hurts me so. _____

You've found _____ some - bod - y new who wants to take my _____
This fool _____ who loves you does-n't want to let you _____

place. _____
go. _____ And there goes my _____ heart _____

breakin' in two. There go my eyes cryin' o-ver you. My arms don't want for us to part. So, when you go, here come the blues, there goes my heart.

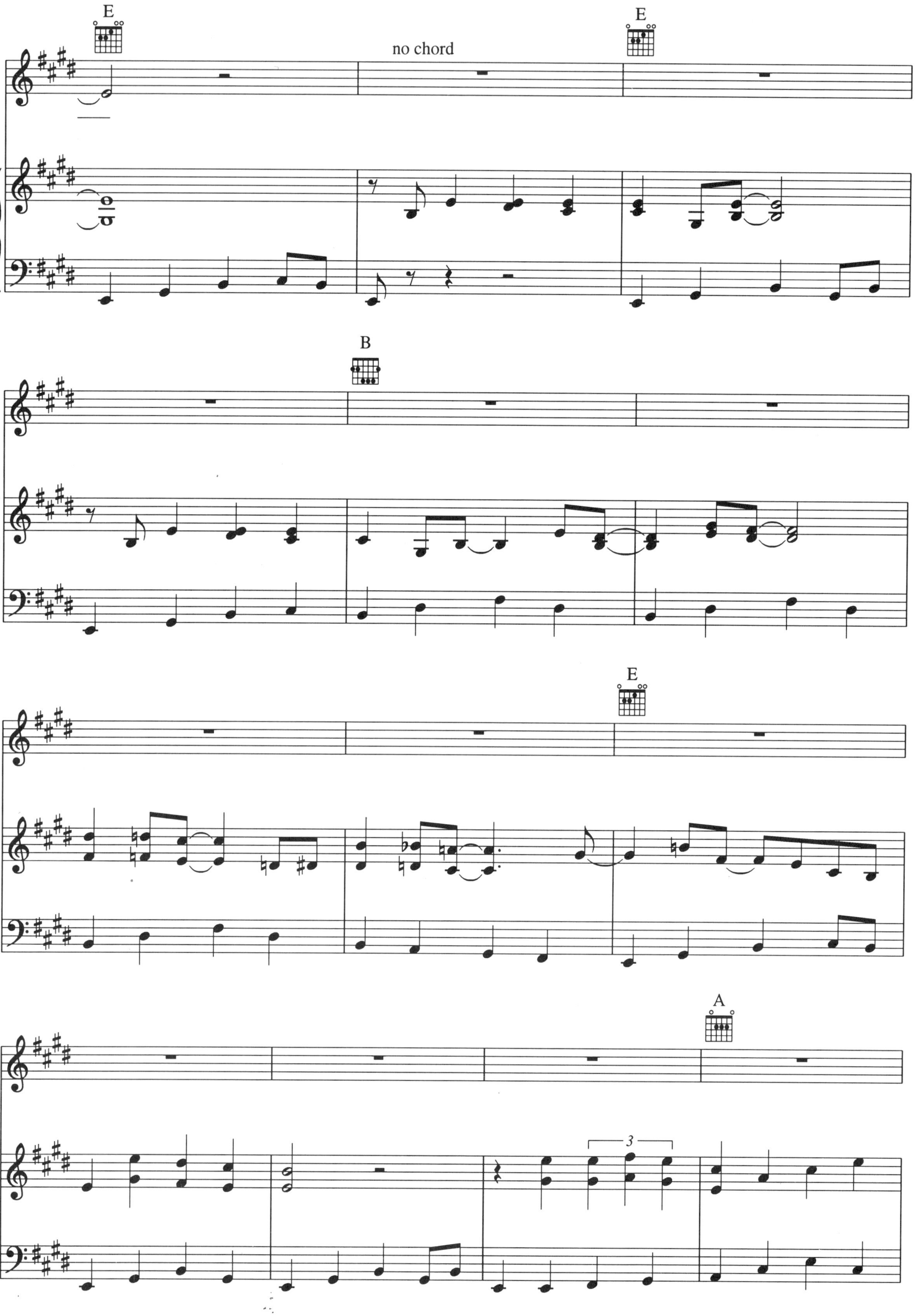
E
no chord
E
B
E
A
3

139

Too Busy Being In Love
Doug Stone

Words and Music by GARY BURR
and VICTORIA SHAW

Moderate Country ballad

If I had tak-en the time to write down a few lines ev-'ry time that you cross
Brand new phras-es ap-pear ev-'ry time you are near. All these words you in-spire

this heart of mine, and put them all in a book,
af-ter all these years, but I nev-er reach for a pen,

how much time would that have took? The words and years have a way of slip-ping by.
break the mood that I'm in. Be-fore I knew it the words were gone a-gain.

© Copyright 1992 by MCA MUSIC PUBLISHING, A Division of MCA INC., GARY BURR MUSIC, INC. and BMG SONGS, INC.
All Rights for GARY BURR MUSIC, INC. Controlled and Administered by MCA MUSIC PUBLISHING, A Division of MCA INC.
International Copyright Secured   All Rights Reserved

MCA music publishing

Bm7 Em7 A D Bm Em
Oh no, well, too bad. There goes the
G A D Bm
chance that I had. I could have
1.,2. writ - ten a play so sweet
3. writ - ten a poem to make young
G A D Bm G A
and so fun-ny, giv-en old Mis - ter Shake-speare a run for his mon-ey,
lov-ers cra-zy. I could have writ - ten a mov - ie for Hep - burn and Tra-cy, and a
Bm F#m7 G D
writ-ten the words to the pret - ti - est tune that would nev - er leave a dry eye
beau - ti - ful song and it starts with your name, writ - ten my way in - to for -

in the room. My only excuse for not do-
- tune and fame, but I have no regrets for not do-
-ing e-nough: well, I was too bus-y
-ing e-nough. Well, I was too bus-y
be-ing in love. Yes, I was too bus-y be-ing in love.

G
D/A
A
2 G
D
A
I was too bus - y
be - ing in love.
D
A7/C♯
Bm7
A
G6
D(add9)/F♯
G
A
D.S. al Coda
Ooo.
I could have
CODA
G
D
I was too bus - y
A
D
Em
be - ing in love.
Ooo,
F♯m
G
D/A
A7
D
hoo.
rit.

TEXAS TORNADO
Tracy Lawrence

Words and Music by
BOBBY BRADDOCK

Moderate ballad

You called me up from Am-a-ril-lo, said you were com-ing to town.
You're ly-ing with me in At-lan-ta, it's such a beau-ti-ful lie.

Copyright © 1993 Sony Tree Publishing Co., Inc.
All Rights Administered by Sony Music Publishing, 8 Music Square West, Nashville, TN 37203
International Copyright Secured   All Rights Reserved

And thought I'd like to tell you, "Hel-lo," and drive an old friend a-round.
You play me like a pi-an-o. I al-ways let you get by.

I pulled up to the air-port, con-fi-dent and cool, but when you stepped off that plane, I knew I was your fool.
I know I'll go through hell, girl, when you find some-one else. But right now I'm in heav-en and I can't help my-self.

My lit-tle

Tex-as tor-na-do, blow-ing me a-way a-gain.

I swore it would-n't hap-pen a-gain. But I

looked at you and then I'm like a

tum-ble-weed in a wild west Tex-as wind.

147

Lyrics:

I swore it wouldn't happen again. But I looked at you and then *(1st time - solo ends)* I'm like a tumbleweed in a wild west Texas wind. You're blowing me away.

Repeat and Fade

UNTANGLIN' MY MIND

Clint Black

Words and Music by MERLE HAGGARD
and CLINT BLACK

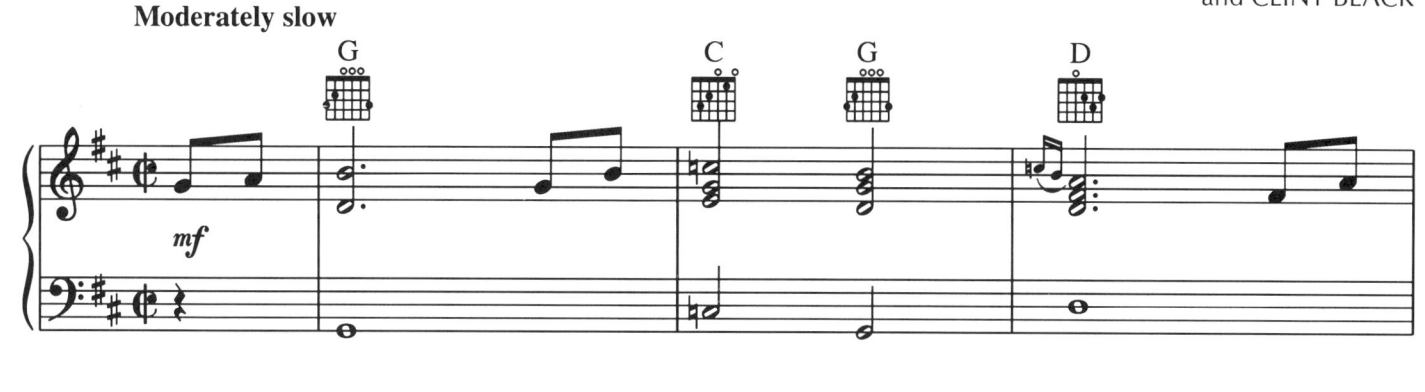

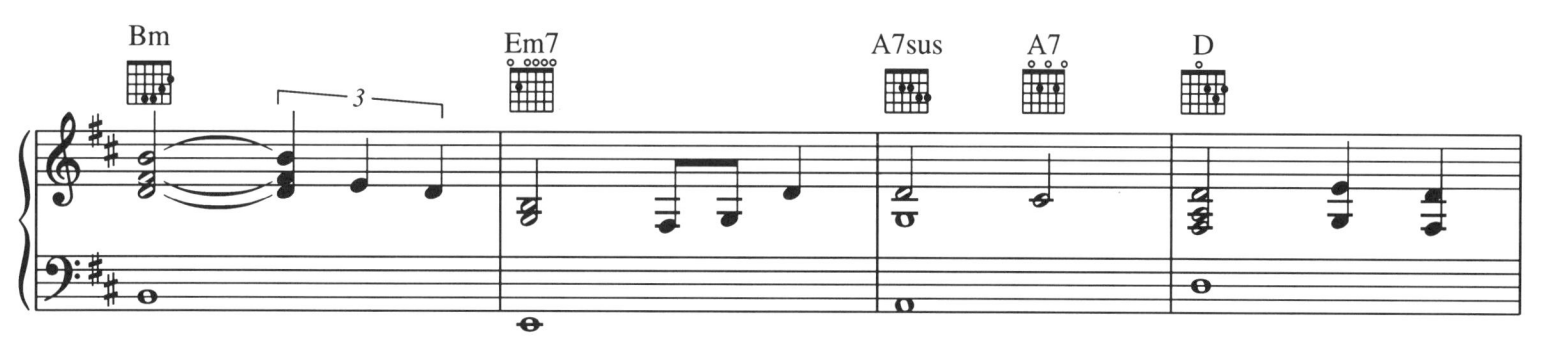

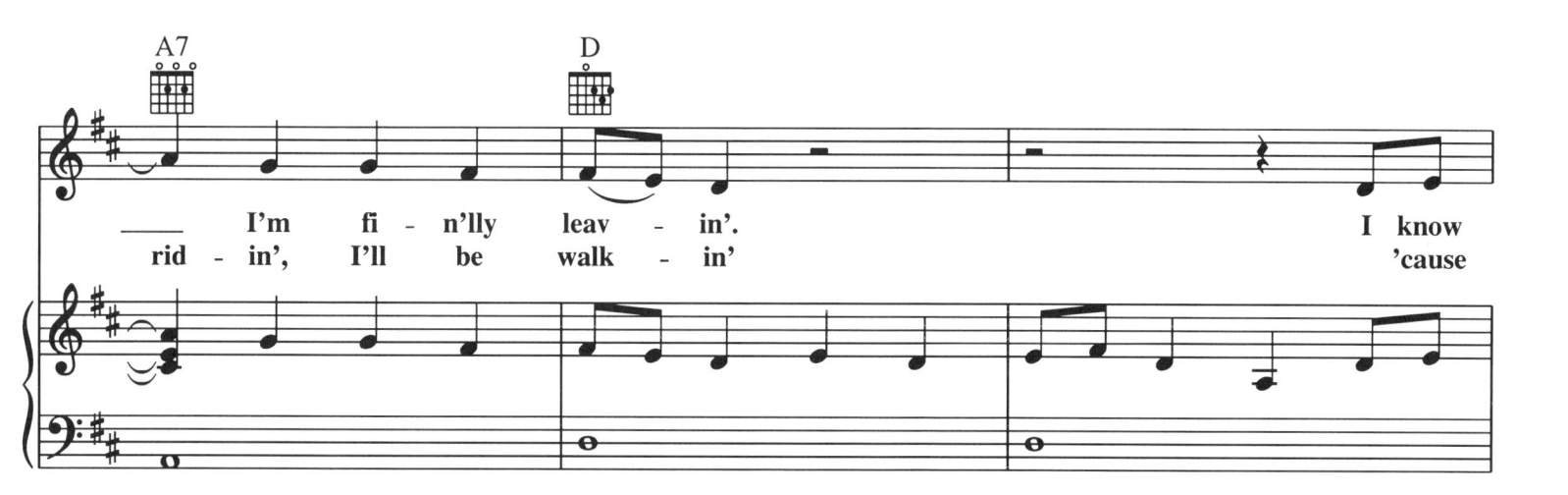

Moderately slow

Well, I guess you're glad to see
tell 'em I won't be

I'm fi-n'lly leav-in'.
rid-in', I'll be walk-in'

I know
'cause

Copyright © 1994 Sony Tree Publishing Co., Inc., Sierra Mountain Music and Blackened Music
All Rights on behalf of Sony Tree Publishing Co., Inc. and Sierra Mountain Music Administered by Sony Music Publishing, 8 Music Square West, Nashville, TN 37203
International Copyright Secured All Rights Reserved

[Sheet music, page 150]

151

the best of me __ is gone.
I __ could-n't stay. __

And I'm sure no one will won-der where __ I've gone to. __ But if an-y-one should ask from time __ to time, tell 'em that you fi-n'lly drove __ me cra-zy __

153

WHAT'LL YOU DO ABOUT ME
Doug Supernaw

Words and Music by
DENNIS LINDE

Moderately fast

All you want-ed was a
Pic-ture their fac-es when you

© 1984 TEMI COMBINE INC.
All Rights Controlled by COMBINE MUSIC CORP. and Administered by EMI Blackwood Music Inc.
All Rights Reserved   International Copyright Secured   Used by Permission

one night stand, the fire of the wine and the touch
try to ex-plain that good ol' boy standin' out

of a man. But I fell in love and ru-ined
in the rain with his nose on the

all of your plans. So, what'll you do a-bout
win-dow pane. Now, what'll you do a-bout

me? I-mag-ine the fac-es on your high class friends when I
me? And what in the world are you plan-nin' to do when a

beat on the door ___ and I get ___ to come in, ___
man ___ comes o - ver just to vis - it with you ___

scream-in', "Come on, ___ love me a - gain." ___ Now,
and I'm on the porch with a 2' by 2'? ___ La - dy,

what-'ll you do ___ a-bout me? Well, you can
what-'ll you do ___ a-bout me? Well, you can

change your num - ber, you can change your name. You can ride ___ like hell ___ on a mid -
call your law - yer, you can call the Fuzz. You can sound ___ the a - larm, wake the

-night train. But that's al-right, Ma-ma,
neigh-bors up. There ain't no way to stop a

that's o-kay. But, what'll you do a-bout me?
man in love. So, what'll you do a-bout me?

158

All you want-ed was a one night stand, the

fire of the wine_ and the touch_ of a man._ But I fell in love,_ so, ba-by, here I am.__ Now, what-'ll you do_ a-bout me?

Well, you can change your num-ber, you can change your name._ You can ride_
call your law-yer, you can call the Fuzz._ You can sound_

__ like hell_ on a mid-night train._ But
__ the a-larm,_ wake the neigh-bors up.__ There

that's al-right, Mama, that's o-kay. But,
ain't no way to stop a man in love. So,

what-'ll you do a-bout me? Well, you can
what-'ll you do a-bout me? Said,

what-'ll you do a-bout me? Said,

what-'ll you do a-bout me?

WORKING MAN'S PH.D.
Aaron Tippin

Words and Music by AARON TIPPIN,
PHILIP DOUGLAS and BOBBY BOYD

In a driving 4

When you get ____ up ev-'ry morn-in' 'fore the sun comes up, toss a lunch box in-to a pick-up truck. ____ A long, hard day sure ain't much fun, but you've got to get it start-ed if you wan-na get it done. You

Copyright © 1993 by BMG Songs, Inc., Mickey Hiter Music, Careers-BMG Music Publishing, Inc. and Acuff-Rose Music, Inc.
International Copyright Secured   All Rights Reserved

set your mind __ and roll __ up your sleeves; __ you're work-in' on a work-in' man's __ P - h. D. __

With your heart __ in your hands and the
When the quit-tin' whis-tle blows and the

sweat on your brow___ you build the things that real-ly make the world_ go a-round. If it
dust set-tles down,_ there ain't no___ troph-ies or___ cheer-in' crowds. You'll

works, if it runs, if it lasts for___ years, you can bet your bot-tom dol-lar it was
face your-self at the end of the day and be damn proud of what-

made right here with pride and hon-or and dig-ni-ty___ from a
ev-er you made. Can't hang it on the wall_ for the world to see_ but you've

man with a work-in' man's_ P - h. D. ___
got your-self a work-in' man's_ P - h. D. ___

Now, there ain't no shame in a job well done from drivin' a nail to drivin' a truck. As a matter of fact, I'd like to set things straight: a few more people should be pullin' their weight. If you want a cram course in real - i - ty, ___ you get your - self a work - in' man's __

P - h. D. ___

YOU'RE GONNA MISS ME WHEN I'M GONE

Brooks & Dunn

Words and Music by KIX BROOKS, RONNIE DUNN and DON COOK

Moderately

I'm still hurting from the last time you walked on this heart of mine.
There's not much chance we're gonna make it if I'm the only one who's trying.
You're good at going through the motions. All I hear are alibi's.

Copyright © 1994 Sony Tree Publishing Co., Inc., Showbilly Music, Buffalo Prairie Music and Don Cook Music
All Rights Administered by Sony Music Publishing, 8 Music Square West, Nashville, TN 37203
International Copyright Secured All Rights Reserved

G
C/G
C
G
I can't find much to be - lieve in.
You know I'm run - ning out of rea - sons
Now I get this emp - ty feel - ing
C/G
C
G
C/G
C
You let me down so man - y times.
and we're run - ning out of time.
when I look in - to your eyes.
G
Am7
Heav - en knows
Some-day, girl,
I don't see
C
how much I love you,
you're gon - na wake up
a love light shin - ing.

but I'm tired of holding on.
and wonder what went wrong.
I don't know what's going on.

You better kiss me,

'cause you're gonna miss me when I'm gone.

To Coda

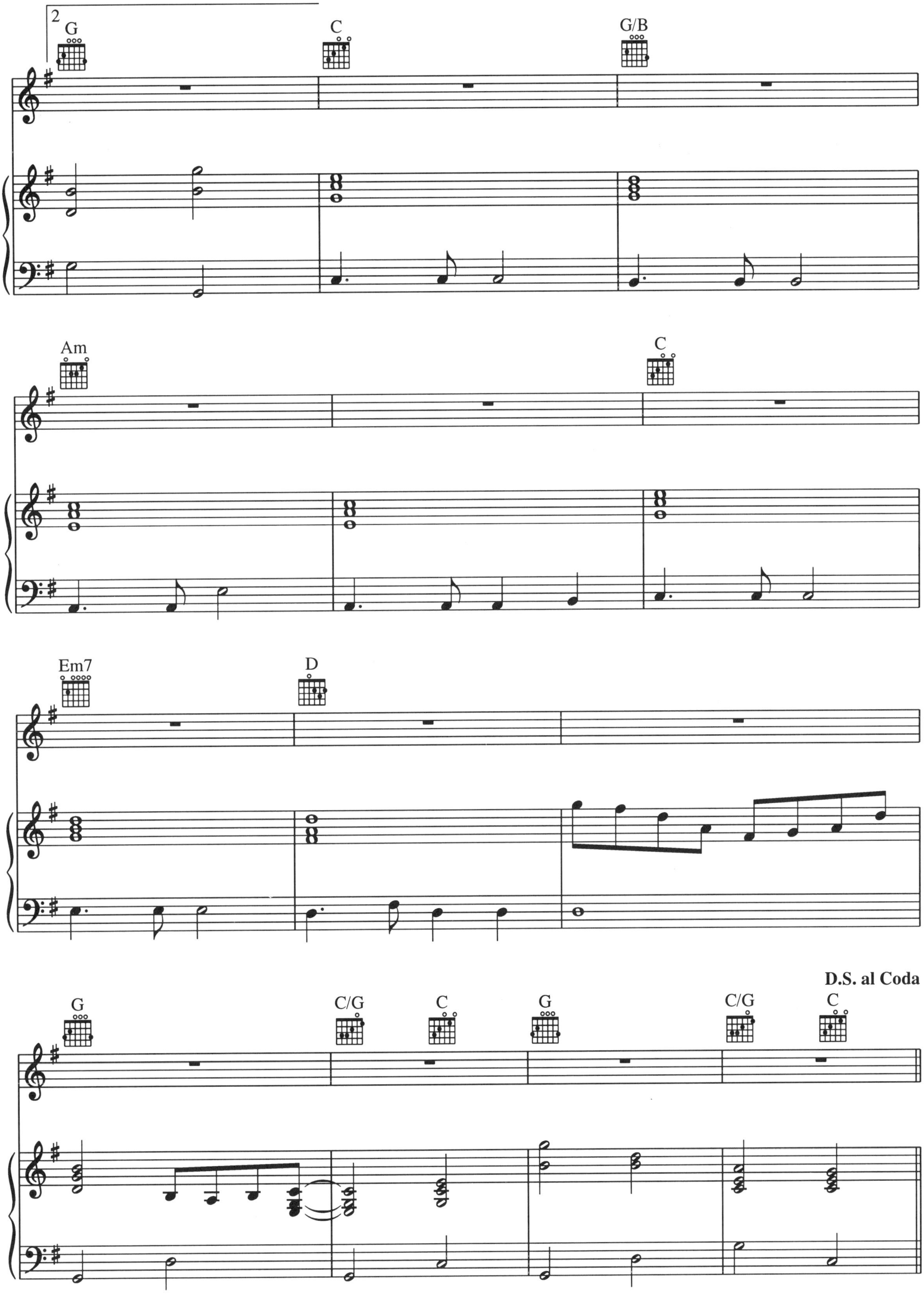
2
G
C
G/B
Am
C
Em7
D
D.S. al Coda
G
C/G
C
G
C/G
C

CODA

You better kiss me, 'cause you're gonna miss me when I'm gone.

Oh, you're gonna miss me when I'm gone.

You better kiss ____ me, 'cause you're gon-na miss ____ me, you're gon-na miss ____ me when I'm gone.

Repeat ad lib. and Fade

You bet-ter kiss ____

YOU AIN'T MUCH FUN
Toby Keith

Words and Music by TOBY KEITH
and CARL GOFF, JR.

Lyrics:

I used to come home late and not a minute too soon, barkin' like a dog, howlin' at the moon. You'd be mad as an

Copyright © 1994 Songs Of PolyGram International, Inc. and Tokeco Tunes
International Copyright Secured   All Rights Reserved

ol' wet hen, __ up all night __ wonderin' where I'd been. __

I'd fall down __ and say, "Come __ help me honey." You

laughed out loud; __ I guess you thought it was funny. But

I've sobered up __ and I got to thinkin', girl, you ain't much fun since I __

quit drink - in'. Now I'm paint - in' the house and I'm
Instrumental solo
fix - in' the sink and I'm mend - in' the fence. I guess I've gone and lost all my
mow - in' the grass and you've made me a list and I'm
good sense. Too much work is
bust - in' my, well... All broke down,
hard for your health. I could - 've died drink - in', now I'm
tail's been drag - gin'. It's a rough old life up

killin' my-self. And I'm feed-in' the dog, sack-in' the trash. It's
here on the wag-on.

hon-ey do this, hon-ey do that. I so-bered up and

I got to think-in', girl, you ain't much fun since I quit drink-in'.

Solo ends Now I'm

CODA

quit drink-in'.

Yeah, I sobered up ____ and I got to think-in', girl, you ain't much fun since I ____ quit drink-in'.